mongoose in chicken

house

&

other poems

henry victor

ISBN: 978-81-8253-167-3

First Edition: 2010
Rs. 100/-

Published by Cyberwit.net
4/2 B, L.I.G. Govindpur Colony,
Allahabad-211004 (U.P.) India
Tel. (91) 09415091004
E-mail: cyberwit@rediffmail.com / info@cyberwit.net www.cyberwit.net

Printed in India.

"IN THE WIDEST DAY,

to find oneself as alone
as in a tight cave
with nothing to lose but this
need to say Nothing."

Brian Chan, *Scratches on the Air*, (2010)

dedicated to

Rt Rev Dr Ken Genge
(former Anglican Bishop in Edmonton)
friend and my colleague in doing theology

&

Dr Iris Devadason
(former professor of English in Bangalore)
friend, and the first to see a poet in me

&

Chandra Victor
(my wife)
friend, and a fellow pilgrim in poetry

About the Author

Henry Victor (whose roots go to Nagercoil, Tamil Nadu, India) was born in Colombo, Sri Lanka where he had his early education. He was ordained an Anglican priest in the Diocese of Colombo in 1974. He then went to India to secure his degrees in Christian Theology and World Religions, moving later to United Kingdom to complete his Ph D.

Prior to settling in Edmonton in July 2000, where he has taught Islamics and World Religions for almost ten years now at the University of Alberta, he worked as a research fellow in Pakistan and been a Professor of Comparative Religion in two of the Sri Lankan Universities - University of Jaffna (Sri Lanka) and Eastern University (Sri Lanka). Henry Victor's academic writings have appeared in refereed journals in Canada and other parts of the world.

Henry Victor's poems have appeared in magazines, journals, and anthologies in Sri Lanka, India, Philippines, United Kingdom, Germany, Sweden, United States and Canada. His collection of poems titled **No Tears** and **Frail Floret** were published in Sri Lanka in 1998 and 1999 respectively. Cyberwit.Net (of India) published Henry Victor's poems in **The Postmodern Temperament: Fifteen Poets** (2003) and **The Ferment of Images** (2004). **Stinging of the Scorpion & Other Poems** (2006) and **Three Faces & Other Poems** (2007) are his most recent collections.

Contents

a highway on my window 1

a prodigal 2

below and beyond 3

bigger dream 4

blocking with pride 5

boasting 6

choose to soar 7

climbing 8

cosmetic compassion 9

crowned to witness 10

dance but touch not 11

disabled soul 12

discerning 13

distant land 14

drowning in doubts 15

dung-beetle 16

emptiness 17

equally tasty 18

escapee 19

extending the stay 20

extreme poverty 21

failure to bloom 22

fasten that gateway 23

feeling the hidden life 24

fifth world 25

fighting fate 26

flight to the south 27

flying from the nest 28

four legged pet 29

game is now over 30

garbage 31

graduating 32

growing and rising 34

holy club 35

hope: merge with the large 36

in garbage 37

irate boatman 38

killing 39

landscaping 40

lay me to rest 41

library book sale 42

living with questions 43

lust for space kills 44

marathon 45

meaning 46

mongoose in chicken house 47

movement 48

my digital frame 49

my psalm forty-two 50

my song 51

mythical dove 52

new life 53

newer journeys 54

predicament 55

prison to pearl 56

psalm twenty-three 57

realism 58

reaping not the return 59

refusal to merge 60

remove not your fence 61

road less traveled 62

sense of life 63

simple pleasures 64

skyscrapers & bigger mosques 65

sneaking away 66

sour grape 67

the missing middle camp 68

the sky pictures 69

the source of peace 70

the stone 71

to bluff 72

to exit 73

today's celebration 74

torment me not with your absence 75

volunteering pain 76

voyaging 77

what is right 78

wild grass 79

yet to evolve 80

a highway on my window

like that little spider
repeatedly slipping
as she climbs
my seven-foot glass window

i slide many times
in my striving to maturity

my tired friend, then sits
and weaves a dream of a highway
to the top with no exit
or, just a fewer exits

ending in a daydream
like that of mine
that heaven with gold paved roads
bought with blood
of a real man
that refused the wide way
a prodigal

reckless
and i continue

a prodigal

first with my lust
running around like a dog in heat
that took me nowhere
except to soreness in soul
and failure in my vocation

next with my love
that wasted self and clearly saw
like a perfect mother
the need for more sacrifice
for another being's becoming

now i'm prodigal in moderation
taking lust and love
in pepper and salt shakers
but now empty and wasted
like that banana peel in the bin

below and beyond

when i lost my soul, i know not
where i dropped it, i remember not

now, for sure, i roam soulless
but with a heavy burden
stepping into every optometrist
in town to enhance my vision of the transcendence
that i may ease my weight in the soulless soul

many have offered cheap advice, quick fixes
and pointed me towards radars
that will teach me to be quickly noticeable

but i'm bent to probe that being
that prompts my becoming
below and beyond all radars
both secular and pretentious

bigger dream

the single bed that sleeps my stiff is warm
under my double blanket
and my body tries to curl
as if it has now returned to my mother's womb

(even as my hand withdraws in
after pushing the clock's button
not so slowly like a snail that pulls in)

disobeying the chiropractor
and my other learned doctor
who had seen my aging indoors
the degeneration in my bone
that requires a careful
straightening even in slumbering

and under that coverlet
my fingers cover my ears, at
the speed of a supersonic jet
that in the secret space of my heart
the call to wellness will not be felt

inside the mantle, at the end, i kill a bigger dream
a vision, like that of lincoln, king, and now, obama
that needs to be dreamed
outside the bedspread, away from a cozy bed

blocking with pride

i exchange my money
for a pricey window curtain
thinking that it will provide
a window of opportunity
for my pride
to be hoisted higher like a flag

but the curtain blocks
those pretty clouds
that you send on my way
through my glassy windows

these clouds, often
come with that silver line
if they end up dark and stormy
transforming my living room
into your school
teaching me to hope
chiselling also my extra conceit

and now, i do not yearn
for a curtain to crane my pride
enjoying what you place
especially your sun that sits inside
my humble span

boasting

colourless boasting
and colourful boasting
like the white and the yolk
in the egg don't mix

the former is health fixing
while the latter tastes well
with potentials to kill
the heart too early

that short man paul from tarsus
chose the first, boasting not of his strength
like the strong north americans do
but his weakness, acknowledging always
the disputes without and fears within

choose to soar

even as i mature more
and my spirit turn stronger
from being a fawn
to a sure-footed deer
i refine my choice

knowing, without any uncertainty
that i can consume
not all that is listed in the menu
every time i walk into an eatery
even if its known for its taste

unlike those days when i tossed in
all that my eyes spotted
and my nostrils smelt
while my hands went on
grabbing towards the greedy self
like that juvenile robin
every exciting experience

i, these days, wait
only for those appropriate
for the soaring of my soul

climbing

the heights people climb to keep its benefit
i was taught, were attained not by sudden flight
but they, while their companions slept
toiled and toiled upward in the night

but in this instant among my generation
i see yet another configuration in operation
that henry longfellow, earlier, failed in his jotting
that smart art of climbing without climbing

cosmetic compassion

the religious clowns spray themselves with perfume
affirming commitment to those in the margin
those with few dollars and a shanty home
looking for free breakfast and few extra change
particularly during festive season

these pseudo godly with bloated egos
sing slyly and pray piously in empty spaces
calling it their spiritual quest
doing nothing, not even moving
a little stone that strengthens
their centre creating that stinky edge

these foxy creatures, with cosmetic compassion
lack an opportunity to stand before a mirror
but bray, unaware their riches are already rotten
with gold and silver too rusted
and their ritual clothes moth-eaten
from the memory of god they will be soon forgotten
they are indeed naked, but see not their nakedness

crowned to witness

my gorgeous kite
that once floated above
(right on top of other kites
less colourful
and much smaller)
is stuck on the crown
of that coconut palm
with string now broken
and entertaining none
but yet witnessing in eternity
to that fragile, frail beauty
of success, short lived

dance but touch not

in a wild brook i saw those awesome fish
that i see normally only in an aquarium
as greed kicked my mind i stooped down
to net some to make my home cheaply colourful

but my quick conscience
battled with self, and battled hard
to make me enjoy that beauty
with lust less eyes
and i returned to my abode
dancing with heart full of swimming fish

disabled soul

i know not why i'm here
i want not to discern
i'm just a robot
like that landed in mars
with no mind of it's own

i keep filling my wallet
i keep grabbing for self
and i pause not to question
that will slow me down
the pace of my seizing more

at the end of my mission
or, when my eyes fail in vision
i know not whether i will be re-cycled
or, dumped to rot
to complete that disintegration

that inbuilt greed
for more, for much more
simple commands
programmed within
disables my soul

discerning

increase in me
the clarity of mind
to discern the nuts and bolts
of authentic service

and let me never be a priest
faithful but foolish
hunting for candle stands
to place it on the altar
and vestments to wear
after the homily has been preached
and the eucharistic prayer
too had been recited
with only a blessing
now to be pronounced
by my transformed living

distant land

i see the world as an airport
huge; flights incoming
with equal number, or even more
flying out
to that beyond destination

but many are not
instead they keep themselves busy
their destination is this world
to work, to make money in the airport
they, very well, know

the others
with great distance to cover
much space to hover
fears they overcome
fixed firmly in hope
on a distinct distant land

drowning in doubts

life, you poured into my cup
overflowing like black coffee
with neither sugar
nor sweetener to sweeten

never did you append
some cream to change colour

there were times i stoically sipped
pretending it tasted like nectar
the drink of gods

and other times, i left coffee to cool
to gulp to give no time for taste
to register in tongue

there were moments, the mug
i hardly approached
philosophizing life beyond pain

or, that living with sting
calling it salvific for soul
but constantly drowning in doubts

dung-beetle

i lack no inspiration
but that comes not with fuel
to adequately excite my will
to spark a fire that starts my soul

to push my destiny in that direction
that i desire to move
actually to fly high, like that eagle
with no spark plugs of aircrafts
or, that of a smaller motor cycle

hence like a dung-beetle i crawl
always backward
far, far from a highway with fear of speed
pushing that piece of dung
into my little cozy tunnel

constantly cherishing
the droppings and depending
on my single skill to smell

emptiness

a million dollar diamond
and a priceless pearl
these were my possessions
as i continued my journey
to that well lit city beyond
with deathless life

i guarded my wealth
even as i passed through hills
and vales to enter the region
with chasmic ravines
crossing breaking ice bridges
often falling and then crawling
and creeping again
to ground that was harder
but only to throw at the end
the two, and myself
jump into that emptiness
never to be heard
never to be reported

equally tasty

guava trees
in greater numbers
and also in variety
i planted in my garden

they bore me fruits
in greater numbers
some readily visible
from the ground

and many
hidden, behind the leaves
but all that same
that delicious taste

and those concealed
among the foliage
were never, and never
of lesser tang

escapee

you were just a few months old
when we bought a dozen of budgies
to keep the house noisy and colorful
it was then, that one of these birds
got out of our aviary
that tore my heart and caused me pain
not because of the loss of my funds
or, the decrease in the sound
but the escapee knew not
to survive in the outside world
marked by too many predators

now, with three months more you to be eighteen
and with your flight away from my sight
the same concern surfaced in my heart
leaving me with a sleepless night

extending the stay

there is lots of work
that needs to be done
before i leave the town

hence i go to the commissioner
of the town council
to let me stay longer
that i may complete task assigned

will he grant me permission
or that permission to delay, deny
i know not today

extreme poverty

my flight is forward
like that of the butterfly
with a broken wing
fluttering around
not far from the water front
beside stanley park
at vancouver, where thousands
ignore my flying
despite my multi-colours

instead, they focus on those seaplanes
landing and taking off
soon to vanish from sight
leaving me, the extreme poverty
alone, to advance
in their space
in my own pace

failure to bloom

my rose shrub
that never blossomed
walked
to my neighbour's bush
to pick the choicest flower
and bore it on her crown
as if her own

while my neighbour's continued
with more colour
and extra fragrance
mine put out more green
increasing
in me a sense of disgrace
and a feeling of failure

fasten that gateway

disobedience is that gateway
ajar to your backyard
that scoundrels use
to make that first contact
with you

once the line is established
you slip to the street
through that gate
and soon you will find
your self in that highway
with plenty of down hills
to enjoy much hustle
soon your dance becomes a rush
to that ultimate crash
your crush with your death

feeling the hidden life

even as you lay napping
with your head on my lap
i, like a blind man touching
put my hand gently
on your bulging belly
revealing that sacred life
bound to bring added laughter
that i lost in my recent struggle
with you, now an assertive daughter

hence, secretly, i name him
with my own name, isaac[1]
that i carried from my father
who, in turn, stole from his
just with a smile

my soul wanting to dance
now takes that leap
to recapture your first smile

and my mind carefully surveys
the many moments
you rested peacefully on my knees
as my eyes behind the eyelids
then, beheld the angel hiding
inside you, a darling daughter
with that life in abundance

---

[1]*The name Isaac means laughter.*

fifth world

earlier i felt i was moving
though at a snail speed
with many genocidal check points
that i dodged daily

so i moved north to move fast
only to loose that inner core
that flesh with nerve to spark fire
in another soul

and now i'm that empty snail shell
blown by the gusting wind
and rolled by the running water
from that melting snow
flowing, constantly towards the great fall
before merging, becoming stagnant
in that superior lake of poverty
the canadian fifth world

fighting fate

i never subjected my soul to fate
always battling a fight

i shaped, and reshaped my destiny
never letting self to settle
to someone else's tune
or my body dance to an alien beat

though i am, now, tempted
i work very hard to let my daughter
too, to fight fate
wanting to fix her destiny

flight to the south

it's still the early fall
soon there will be snowfall
the birds are flying south
while i sit by the valley to watch
those escaping the cold
also those cliques too hard
into which it's difficult
to easily melt

flying south
i saw a single bird
may be, still a juvenile
with a sense of hesitant
but a flight also jubilant

will she make it lord
without you sending guardians to guard
from evil that may shoot her down

flying from the nest

i know you must fly from that nest
that housed your body and soul
for those eighteen long years
from which you always looked out
while your mum and i kept
that constant flying in, to protect
and strengthen every feather
in your wings to take off one day to find
a partner to make your own nest

in that process of my constant flying in
for such an enormous extended time
i have lost my sight beyond that nest
in which i also had lost my soul
that cradled your most beautiful being
making all my flying and fruit gathering
now, utterly meaningless, tearing my heart
multiplying my tears to endlessly flow
while i struggle, in my mind, to let you go

four legged pet

tina, i adopted
paying a price
that i consider a way too higher
for her breed
but to provide a companion
to my only daughter
i counted no cost

tina, as she grew older
preferred her freedom
not only to choose her food
but also her company
until she did end up pregnant
with quads
leaving not my home

tina's kids were clean
filling belly with warm milk
enjoying also the mum's embrace
until they did grow
to choose to sup the dirt
foretelling also a blueprint
of another growth

game is now over

statements taken out of context
twisted and perverted truths
half-truths, lies, and more blatant lies
woven together with graphs and hard numbers
enhancing the appearance of objectivity
to make the unsigned written statements
sometimes contradicted and at other
corroborated between the accusers
that accused to condemn, also assassinate
the character of a person, nay, themselves

the game, in any case, is now over
i must be quick to re-pack my bag
with jersey, sweat socks and boots
to be on my way home

scores are unimportant
performance is irrelevant
for sure, i kept my calm
and did not collapse

my wife that last refuge and comfort
will anxiously wait with hot chocolate
that i may drink to sleep tonight in peace
to journey tomorrow into another calvary

garbage

two separate loads of garbage
i carry to tip at the dump
one in black to rot
the other in blue with a potential
to rotate before i, myself, perish

graduating

she now knows love
love, not a lifeless thing
that she used to talk about those days
while carrying a backpack
full of books and binders

a mustang she wanted to drive
symbol of success and speed
a perfect blend with boom
and the ooze of black-gold

but today for her
only one thing that matters
living with a man
sharing his failure
to graduate from a high school

that teaches not techniques
to survive that stoppage
of an upward movement
and a free flow of more

her achievement
she carries with care
as if holding the first university degree
that will open the greater door
to a doctorate
to walk around with a prefix
before her name

now she smiles, inside
every time she feels that kick
a little stretching

in that cozy cave
intricately decorated convocation hall
calling him, her baby
while feeling that wall, outside

her boy will soon graduate
to enjoy her love
her success, her own graduation
to that new title – mum

growing and rising

hardly any roots
in my mammillaria cacti
the specific name of it, to me
remains unknown; but growing
beautifully and taller

i have seen a few pink blooms
now and then, some last year too
four new bulbs in addition
have grown from that one
i brought in seven years ago

my attempt to separate a tuber
to grow as a separate plant
did not work
but i saw healthy milky sap
lot of life, that energy within

that hope is mine too
still rootless in this soil
and my name much unknown
i crave to continue my rising
with that milky sap, life within

holy club

that *tremendum mysterium*
the sense of holy, i saw
i sensed strongly around
hence i joined that club
named: holy catholic church
wheeling and dealing on holy

and i saw them bathing
in the river
walking further
the upstream i dipped
myself in clean water
returning i found
myself out of that club

hope: merge with the large

money, always, easily slipped
through my fingers
lands that i tried to own also slid
quickly from my hand

the bed i slept in the night
someone else secretly
occupied in the day

the juvenile bird i cuddled
in my bosom
to give warm comfort and a nest
flew away to build her own

my remains too, soon
the fire will consume
leaving, perhaps, my soul
to merge with that larger soul
that welcomingly smiles
from behind the veil

in garbage

hardly ever i saw an umbrella
those days in garbage
they were strong and large
and i paid a little more

less i pay today
for small
and smaller ones
in many fancy colours

soon in plenty
to be dumped
with hardly
after one, or two use

none are there today
to carefully hem
black thread tight
for a long and a longer use

i also see peter, paul
and more in hub mall
with degrees, universities churned
as if fish, factories canned
but with expiry dates before time

irate boatman

i see the lonely boatman pulling his boat
to the banks of the river
he cruised only for a shorter moment
shorter than that summer in far north

the yachter appeared exhausted
and even frustrated
while the river continued her dance
her fast flowing towards the ocean

the boatman did not begin his boating
from that little point the river began, or dropping
dangerously many suicidal heights, and suddenly
spreading thinly on grounds a boat could ground

now the retired oarsman like jonah[1] is envious
that the river that carried him continues
without him and his tiny craft
before merging into a oneness with the wide sea

---

[1] *It is a reference to the Hebrew prophet of the Bible. My reading of the little book suggests this "minor prophet was petty and envious of God's universal love to save all including the non-Hebrew people of Nineveh!*

killing

stomping, hard, on it
i killed the silver fish
innocent
that didn't come to hurt

but my superior weight
on my boot
just squashed it
for no apparent reason

except, that i am a human
with superior right
to decide on life and death
in this anthropocentric universe

where i have, already, murdered
the creator
of the silver fish
to create him in my own image

landscaping

the yard around my new house
needed landscaping
and i hired some ex-filipinos
to fix the top soil that they spread
so liberally with their tagalog[1]
that the caucasian surveyor
following them
found it too high in some spots
and too low in others
to pass the test of the city inspector
a real turkey in his breed
leaving me surveying the sky
for more manna to be dropped
before i covered it with sod

---

[1]*Tagalog is one of the many languages listed in the Ethnologue of the Philippines.*

lay me to rest

do i envy those who pass
from life to death
with that certainty of eternity
a greater mansion to occupy

do i carry sympathy for those
who lack in life that faith
that alleged passport to the beyond
with a send off from a chapel here

many questions my mind may probe
but, for sure, i have informed my wife
and our daughter: that none
from holy club sprinkle phoney poetry

instead my simple frame
be laid to rest naked in a quick flame
with no words that my mind
shall be burdened to interpret

library book sale

million people i saw
with their visions boxed
later carted, and piled on tables
in the underground car park

they were in no particular order
and now they were going cheap
to make room for others
maybe younger and relevant

the million now will go to foster homes
to provide a company in couch
or to be abused before discarded
like that condom, good for nothing

my dream within, now shudders
and hesitates to flow through my finger
to rise up as a poem, a genii
to serve another soul in need of an insight

living with questions

from this fringe theatre
my exit should have been long ago
but the reason, or reasons
for that delay i know not

despite my failure
to entertain the masses
or, educate the elites in the edge
none have pushed me to close shop

now that the clock is turned back
am i expected to perform
a new trick or, that old
continuing with a little tinkering
lost even the sour savour

grafted mango plantlet
in my mother's land
grew into a young sturdy tree
bearing fruits of diverse size, shape
and taste in her different limbs
but all sweet as nectar

as i walked into my middle age
and more, she has outgrown me
now, allowing hardly any fruits
not even those sour ones
for pickling to add some savour
on days when my food is bland

lust for space kills

little less than eleven
hundred square feet
housed comfortably
the three of us

and after the one
who took the most space
in that cozy house
decided to fly away

the remaining found
lust too cramped
in that tiny heart

hence they set up
that more than twenty-two
hundred square feet

ending with, that strain
to pump blood
threatening to stop
to prematurely kill

marathon

i now train my self
with more shorter snooze
for the marathon sleep
that some mistakenly call death

i practice also that perfect, infinite
silence of that granite
transforming my transient soul
the red rose into a perfect fossil

that at the closing stage
i fail not to easily merge
with that deathlessness
of my death, the dreamless sleep

meaning

those events, joys and pains
that you send on my way
are designs that you, the unseen artist
scratch, sketch and etch
that i may ponder in my heart
the secret intentions of that invisible artist
but never am i permitted
to publicly interpret
to proclaim
the meaning of artistic events
making me a mute
in the very presence of your absence

mongoose in chicken house

my wife and i woke early in the dawn
by the noise inside
from our chicken house beside
my mother's house i now own

i did move fast
and my wife too came at last
to see a mongoose enjoying the feast
of our chicken

now blinded by the laser light
from red eyes of the evil beast
that made me too, hesitate
to pick up a stick, to take revenge on a brute

movement

in my present life cycle
that they call *samsara* in south asia
i live, move and have my being
as if i am that piece of spatial rock
moving around, speedily
in the outer orbit of this planet
but with no sense of urgency

from where this junk came
or, into which new phase
this will reincarnate
if i were to collide with
a purpose-filled satellite
or, how long this track will last
i have no clue except a clouded mind

my digital frame

from his infinite mega memory
pictures of rare beauty change constantly
in my white four feet by four feet
digital frame fixed firmly on my wall

and yet i rarely greet him running away
too quickly to pick up a channel
that my worn out wallet provides with pain
increasing unnecessary storms within my soul

with it i reject the poise
the pictures offer freely

my psalm forty-two

as the cacti on my window sill
keeps turning towards the sun
the very source of her growth
to grow with bentness and flowering

my soul too yearns
for your invisible presence
to be intoxicated
and also distorted

early morning i seek your face
in the ancient word
the lees and scum
my ancestors have left behind

and as i step out of my door
i feel your formless feature
in every neighbour i encounter
or consciously ignore

settling down in the evening
confidently i say, what matters
is not my seeing, but being seen
by that one who watches my night

my song

santa claus has walked into that closed box
with no opening from inside
he is trapped and suffers much with claustrophobia

who misled him
why to him, did this happen

i wake up at five
and roll in bed till seven
sip coffee till nine
my breakfast at ten
protesting against heaven
even beyond eleven
that my life is too short

jingle bells have gone too long
too much fun and no pain
though my garment is always red
with that i also wear my white beard
pretending to be very old and wise
repeating the same christmas song

mythical dove

picking up my shoe
i walked to hit, to kill
the cockroach
hovering under my table
like a fighter helicopter

even as my horror
and anger ascended
i saw a dove-like bird
that descended
and picked the roach
before it multiplied
its kind, a nuisance
and in my heart
the sense of annoyance

new life

i saw clean and fast running water
i would not hesitate to name it river
so i bent down
and washed, with my wife
our daughter's soiled clothing
making them perfectly spotless

and my daughter
in dirt-free clothes
left home on her own
to attend a new school
for an authentic learning
a new lease for a renewed life

newer journeys

my body, that machine
circulates fuel not so well
threatening, frequently, to stop
or, permanently shut down
certain sections
to slow down my soul
or, to suggest, with force, a path
my spirit never planned

this prompted me
to turn to a mechanic
for whom my soul is irrelevant
and who considers not the dream
that my sprit secretly dreams

adding tubes to that machine
but from within
the mechanic who touches not
any grease, nor the lubricating oil
made my soul soar higher
and higher to spaces my spirit
has never journeyed

predicament

i am reluctantly ready
for an exit; this life to quit
darkness, or light in that womb
next that i should now enter
that i will know not

i am tired of politeness
far removed from the real
that buries me alive like an avalanche
burying that enthusiast of speed
and winter sport in the remote rockies

soon will be forgotten those doings
of compassion i squeezed into a larger mug
that they may relish as they cherished
the lanka lion lager[1] in that island of conflict
such is my predicament

---

[1]*Lion Larger is a brand of beer brewed in Sri Lanka.*

prison to pearl

i am –
no, we are
for no longer i feel alone
strangely, there is togetherness
that surrounds me
wrapping me with warmth
and increasing in my soul that poise
the quietness in my heart
sense of comfort in mind –

we are
trapped and imprisoned
with cunning motions
and crafty resolutions
that the so called crazy
democracy
the seven blind
from the seventy dumb
weave together
through sly scheme
like the spider web

but we
like that trapped
raindrop grow
gradually into a pearl
of great price
that could neither be destroyed
nor ignored
waiting in our prison
for forty years like mandela
to guide the nation
that had bled for too long

psalm twenty-three

you with blatant disregard for certainty
have made me a sure slave of eternity
despite my constant and unsuccessful
revolts against your shepherding, control

you make me walk in your garden
with chaotic colours in which my eyes
see disorder with patches of randomly planted
vegetables and herbs unsuitable to my taste buds

you expect me to see life, life of victory
in demolitions, destructions and in exilic slavery
where opportunities one by one evaporates
like the quickly melting winter snow

but did i hear you whispering, in my ears, thanks
when i cursed you and confirmed yours as messy mess
with much disregard to your making meaning
in your own terms, your space and moment

realism

i fail not to feel the bitter cold
to see that excruciating pain
the pitch darkness of wintry long nights
soothing only for those who like bears
know that knack of hibernating

i refuse not to hear that whining
deep within my bleeding heart
acknowledging also my stupidity
inherited as well as that from my *karmic*
accumulation of frequent misbehaviour

my inclination is for a set of telescopical
eyes of the eagle that can both soar higher
and dive deeper with courage
into that abysmal crater rather than create
unrealistic computer constructions, or deconstructions

there is greater character, i know for certain
in seeing november as the month before december
than in the name of the power of positive thinking
distorting the real, considering the month
after halloween as the early spring

reaping not the return

is it my tightfistedness
that you punish
by taking away from me
that which fills my heart

i had many other things
to fight for to safe guard self
when you broke open
my home, my soul to steal

today I have no more
energy to battle
my destiny that brings
me, hardly any delight

i ploughed the field
and with my own hands removed rocks
to plant seed, and watered it with sweat
but to harvest, someone else you sent

refusal to merge

my smaller, marginal 'i' refuses that merging
with that larger 'we' that is part of the still larger
and unlimited, ever expanding elastic cosmos embracing
the little 'i' as the ocean readily cuddles the rain drop

and my little revolts, then, are speedily stated
in my careful scrubbing of the tiny oil drop
on my driveway, left behind by my daughter's car
that has just pulled out from my parking spot

and also on my spraying lysol, on my toilet seat
every time my friend pays a social visit to my abode
as if he has left a graffiti on the wall like a restless teen
protesting that we grow

remove not your fence

discipline is a fence
remove that, you will see
the miscreants walking, first
in your backyard
and soon in your bedroom
with you in warm embrace
unable to let them go
at least, until
you are pregnant with two
or, even more

this lesson i learnt
from tina, my daughter's first pet
dog, that later died of cancer

road less traveled

assist me to float
on the waves of your ocean
rather than swim
in my own direction

guide me to glide
on the wings of your angel
instead of choosing to fly
in heights not so detrimental

direct me in your route
even if it is hilly and snaky
lest i choose my lane
of ease beyond risk

sense of life

prince is pushed out
to become an outcast
cause: they say, destiny
or, dictated by fate

without dreaming
but by a simple commitment
to an act of little kindness
the kingdom is again thrust
on that, now, drunken outcast

an act of courage
a matter of fate
an intense debate
fills my mind
but never i find
the true sense of life
except in an act of little kindness

simple pleasures

a strong cup of coffee
that plain black
with nothing added into it

a shorter story
to explore the collapse
of my strong youthful dreams

and a simple seat
to consume the free providence
of the strong morning sun

these are what I seek
these days in the dusk
of my crumbling life

that missed
those many birds in hand
with its focus on one in bush

skyscrapers & bigger mosques

depression in small children
and obsession with paediatric drugs
embarrass health services
that keep busy world-wide
where people are extremely
self-centred with no time
even for leisure and push
the spousal relationships
to the backseat
making loyalty evaporate
but building, steadily, buildings
including skyscrapers
and bigger mosques
while i see and sense
with that third eye
an increasing impatience of people

sneaking away

like a little squirrel
you slipped with such ease
easily into my being
with a smile
that mesmerized my soul

in that effortlessness
of swallowing you into my heart
i failed to notice the ache
of that womb
that you already had tattered
towards your liberty

and i also did not realize
that with that same ease
you would, one day, slip away
like siddhartha sneaking away
causing much anguish
but this time to my mind
impregnated with an elevated dream

it was with that same smile
you slid
into another embrace, while
i, now, sit and meditate
the meaning of that beam
while you, out the corner of your eyes
measure the rising flood level
of my disillusion

sour grape

two errors, like two worms into that bud
crept into my perception
the one, me mistaking
you, my baby, to be an angelic being

while the other, mistaking a heavenly loan
as if you were an outright grant
that i need not return

these satanic worms becoming dormant
but only for a shorter moment
transformed you into an inedible fruit
that sour grape

from which i am
like that fox, forced now
to walk away empty handed

the missing middle camp

shopping malls i kept away from
then, and even now
but for reasons so poles apart
like a valley and a tall mount

then it was my submerging
in surface sensuality and sexuality
but now it's a struggle to climb
the steeper height of spirituality

but what i lacked
always, is that middle camp
that between the vale and the hill
a moderation in intoxication

the sky pictures

it is his paintings that i see
in the east and the west
in the north and the south

he paints non-stop
mixing colours and simply splashing
on the canvas

in the blindness of my soul
coupled with greed for more
i seldom pause to view the sky pictures

the source of peace

while driving back to fairview
i was, very strangely, relaxed
i stopped a few times
just to watch the sky
to enjoy the beauty
and to let the colours of the sky
make imprints on my mind
while i also clicked a few digital prints

on quiet reflection
i saw the source of paint with varied shades
as the rising sun
but an overcast, like a dominating woman
who refusing joy to those around
swallows all tints that hint at greater peace
with grace

the stone

i wondered
who would roll the stone for me
but the angel
stood beside the rolled stone with a smile
welcoming my gratefulness

i wondered, again
who would roll the stone for me
but the master
motioned me to roll the stone for him
thanking me not for my services

to bluff

ants around my house
do not go on hikes
to dark and quiet spots
to gaze at the vastness
the milky way
and that beyond
to smell their smallness
and be comfortable

they have no need
to sense the presence of god
to craft a religious system
to bluff, to exploit another

to exit

i struggle to learn that art
from day-dream to exit

that highway of high speed
to the real world of small pace
with strip malls, gas stations
schools, and many more
with a home to feed
my body, mind, heart and soul

with science to weave the real vision
like that summer spider
performing that humble task
of building a web far
far from that limelight
the hustle and bustle of the market

in that sacred space
where silence leads to peace
with the end of all rat race

today's celebration

hundreds, maybe thousands
those bright yellow dancing dandelion heads
along my narrow winding, walking trail
last week bragged, heartily, their pride and hardiness
their ability to withstand contempt and ridicule of others

but this week they are soft balls
like men and women adorned with white hair
and soft limbs in extended care
ready to fly away with just one shot
that one blow, or even a soft kick

today they celebrate their pride of yesterday
may be, may be they believe in reincarnation
or, in resurrection like that of the despised man
from the early day nazareth

torment me not with your absence

despite my running away for decades four
my absence from your grace
you, to enable me to sublimate
my ever-flowing, limitless libido
the cause of the ill impact of your grace
you still visited me in that smiling baby
of course, causing also guilt to another
teaching me, an old dog, new tricks
with which to hound you, the hound of heaven
hounding me, before and beyond, those forty years

but, again, i have fallen from your mercy
that was short lived in my life
making me now, to wander
as a mad dog looking for one more
piece of bone, seeing that smiling face
your earlier grace that i may peep at you just once

hence now i drive to the west, then to east
looking also in south, sweeping your space from north
beyond leduc and millet, the city and the hamlet
while you torment me with your absence

volunteering pain

misinterpreting a smile i volunteered
to drink the cup of pain yet to come
for at that moment i was bent on that intent
of, only, escaping a present pain

hence all those abrasions i again
misinterpreted, calling them maturing
like the rough barks of the huge tree
so that i might continue, steadily, branching
never noticing the death of little grass
under my shade until a desert
had surrounded my volunteer living

voyaging

three voyagers were we
in that small boat
rowing in the rough seas

it was then one died
but me the captain
and my co-captain
agreed not to let the corpse
sink to bottom of the ocean

so we carried the dead body
in yacht with the stink
stinging in heart
as the seafaring continued
with great pain

what is right

ee cummings
has come and gone
ts eliot too
but right is still very elusive
and hollow
very lyrical too